Aesop's Fables

The Lion and the Mouse
&
Other Fables

 Retold by Andrea Stacy Leach
Illustrated by Holly Hannon

Paradise
Press, Inc.

The Fables

The Lion and the Mouse 4

The Frogs Who Desired a King 8

The Boy Who Cried Wolf 11

The Dog in the Manger 14

The Lion and the Mouse

A mouse, feeling playful, ran up a sleeping lion's nose. The lion, angry to be awakened from his nap, caught the mouse between his big paws and prepared to kill him.

"Please, mighty King of Beasts, do not kill me," the mouse pleaded. "If you spare my life, I will never forget it. A day may come when I can do the same for you."

The lion smiled and let the mouse go, thinking it funny that so small an animal could ever be of help to him.

But one day the lion was caught in a net that a hunter had set for him. The lion let out a loud roar that was heard throughout the forest. The mouse recognized the lion's roar and came to his side at once.

"You thought I was joking," the mouse said to the lion.

"But now I can return the favor you gave me." He chewed on the net with his sharp teeth until the lion was free from the hunter's net.

No act of kindness, however small, is wasted.

The Frogs Who Desired a King

The frogs lived in a large pond, where they played and splashed about all day long.

But some were not content to live this easy life. They cried to the frog god, "Send a king to rule over us, so we may know what to do."

The frog god was amused by their request, and he threw a large log into the middle of the pond. The frogs were afraid of the new log king and ran away to hide.

Soon, they realized their log king was not at all powerful. In fact, it did not even move. The frogs grew bold and hopped right on top of it.

"Give us a proper king," the frogs complained to their god. "We want one who will rule over us."

But now the frog god was angry at the frogs for not being satisfied with what had been given to them. So he sent a stork to the pond to gobble up the frogs.

Let well enough alone.

❧ 10 ❧

The Boy Who Cried Wolf

The shepherd boy watched his sheep in the hills above the village. He was often lonely because no other people were around.

One day he decided that he needed company. He began crying, "Wolf! Wolf!" at the top of his lungs.

The villagers, thinking a wolf had attacked the sheep, ran into the hills to help. When they arrived, they did not see a wolf, but the boy enjoyed his trick— and the villagers' company.

The next day, the boy felt lonely again, so he cried, "Wolf! Wolf!" And as before, the villagers came to rescue the sheep and found no wolf.

Then, one day, a wolf really did come to attack
the sheep. The boy again cried, "Wolf! Wolf!" But the
villagers were tired of being tricked. They paid no
attention to the boy and went on with their work.

The wolf had a tasty meal as the boy ran away in fright.

Liars are not believed, even when they tell the truth.

The Dog in the Manger

One day a dog was looking for a place to take a nap. He saw a manger full of hay and decided that it would make a good bed.

As he was pawing the hay into a pile, he got a piece in his mouth. "Phooey!" the dog said, spitting out the hay. "How can anyone eat something so dry and tasteless?" And he settled down for a nap.

The dog tossed and turned but he could not fall asleep. "This hay is worthless. It makes me itch," he complained. But the dog stayed in the manger, too lazy to move.

At the end of the day's work, the ox went to her manger to get some hay for dinner. She found the dog there and politely asked him to move so she could get to the hay. But the dog snapped, "Leave me alone, you old ox!"

The ox tried to eat the hay several more times. But each time the dog growled and snapped at her. Finally the ox said, "You cannot eat the hay or use it for a bed, but still you will not let me enjoy it. You're mean and selfish."

Some will not let others have what they cannot enjoy themselves.